Problem-Solving Skill Sheets

Level A
Blackline Masters

Carole Greenes
George Immerzeel
Earl Ockenga
Linda Schulman
Rika Spungin

DALE
SEYMOUR
PUBLICATIONS
P.O. BOX 10888
PALO ALTO, CA 94303

Editor: Elaine Murphy
Production Coordinator: Ruth Cottrell
Illustrator: Dick Davies
Cover Designer: Terry Eden
Compositor: WB Associates
Printer: Malloy Lithographing

ISBN 0-86651-087-7

Order Number DS01291

cdefghi-MA-89321098

DALE
SEYMOUR
PUBLICATIONS
P.O. BOX 10888
PALO ALTO, CA 94303

INTRODUCTION

TOPS (Techniques of Problem Solving) is a comprehensive program for the development of problem-solving skills and strategies. It has been designed to complement existing mathematics textbook programs. TOPS has instructional materials for the primary, elementary, junior high, and high school levels. At the primary level, there is a *problem-solving kit* that provides an introduction to problem solving. At the elementary level, there are *student workbooks* which provide instruction, reproducible *skill sheets* which provide problem-solving maintenance and practice, and *problem card decks* and *transparency masters* which provide enrichment. At the junior high level, there are blackline master *skill sheets* for developing and reinforcing problem-solving skills, and both *problem card decks* and *transparency masters* for enrichment. At the high school level, there are two different *problem card decks* and two different sets of *transparency masters* for problem-solving practice and enrichment. Together, these materials provide the core for a program in one of the most important of mathematical areas—problem solving.

For each grade level, grades 3–6, there is a set of 64 reproducible skill sheets. The skill sheets are organized into four calendar units with 16 sheets per unit. This organization ensures that the computational skills and concepts required already have been introduced to students.

PROBLEM-SOLVING SKILL SHEETS: LEVEL A

The Level A skill sheets provide practice with choosing the operation; finding and using data presented in graphic displays such as tables, pictures, and stories; making drawings; guessing and checking; and using logic. The following chart shows the number of skill sheets provided for each skill or strategy within any calendar unit.

PROBLEM-SOLVING SKILL OR STRATEGY	CALENDAR UNIT				TOTAL
	I	II	III	IV	
Choosing the Operation	6	6	6	6	24
Finding Facts	6	6	6	6	24
Making Drawings	1	1	1	1	4
Guessing and Checking	2	2	2	2	8
Using Logic	1	1	1	1	4

Although the skill sheets are numbered sequentially, they need *not* be completed in that order. They may be selected as needed to provide practice, maintenance, or extension of ideas and skills originally presented in the TOPS Level A developmental workbooks, *Choose the Operation: Addition and Subtraction* and *Choose the Operation: Multiplication and Division,* or in the class textbook.

USING TOPS: A TOTAL PROBLEM-SOLVING PROGRAM

If you have the developmental workbooks, reproducible skill sheets, and problem card decks, we recommend that they be used in the following manner. The developmental workbooks, *Choose the Operation: Addition and Subtraction* and *Choose the Operation: Multiplication and Division*, each should be completed within a two- or three-week period of time. In addition, one period each week of the year should be devoted to problem solving, both practice and enrichment. Students should complete and discuss one or two skill sheets and three or more problem cards during each of these periods.

OBJECTIVES

LEVEL A PROBLEM-SOLVING SKILL SHEETS

SOLVING PROBLEMS

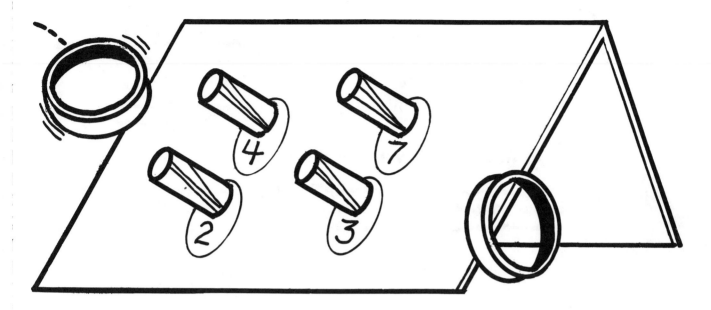

Solve each problem.

1. Dirk got 4 on one throw.
He got 2 on the other throw.
What was his total score?

_____

2. Kay got 2 on one throw.
She got 7 on her other throw.
What was her total score?

_____

3. Jill made a total score of 5 with 2 throws.

She got _____ on one throw and

_____ on the other.

4. Leon made a total score of 6 on two throws.

He got _____ points on each throw.

MAKING DRAWINGS

1. Mr. Pulaski saw 4 large sailboats.
Each large sailboat had 2 sails.
Mr. Pulaski also saw 2 small sailboats.
Each small sailboat had 1 sail.
How many sails were there altogether?

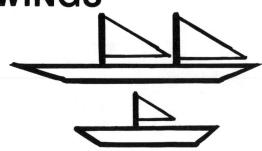

Make a drawing to help you answer the question.

Show the sails on each boat.

Large Boats   Small Boats

Count the sails.

There are _____ sails altogether.

SOLVING PROBLEMS

Solve each problem.

1. Louis and Howard made pancakes. Louis used 3 cups of flour. Howard used 2 cups of flour. How many cups of flour did they use in all?

_____

2. Howard put 9 blueberries into his pancake mix. Louis put 9 blueberries into his pancake mix. How many blueberries did they use altogether?

_____

3. Louis made 8 large pancakes. He made 6 small pancakes. How many pancakes did Louis make altogether?

_____

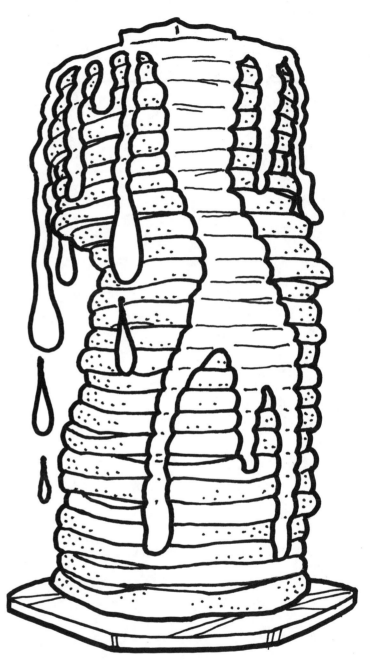

4. Howard made 4 pancakes for himself. He made 5 pancakes for his brother. How many pancakes did Howard make?

_____

5. Louis ate 2 large pancakes and 6 small pancakes. How many pancakes did Louis eat?

_____

USING LOGIC

1. Who is the winner?

Draw a circle around the people wearing glasses.

Draw a box around the people wearing hats.

The winner is
- wearing glasses.
- wearing a hat.

The winner is _____.

The winner has a box and a circle.

2. Which prize fits the clues?

The prize has
- wheels.
- doors.

The prize is _____.

4

Name _____

SOLVING PROBLEMS

Solve each problem.

1. Sarah had 9 posters. She gave 3 posters to her brother. How many posters does she have left?

_____

2. Kelly made 12 glasses of lemonade. She sold 8 glasses. How many glasses did she have left to sell?

_____

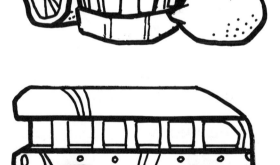

3. There were 15 people on the bus. Eight of the people got off the bus. How many people were still on the bus?

_____

4. Gail had 13 Superman comic books. She gave 9 of them to Frank. How many Superman comic books does she have left?

_____

5

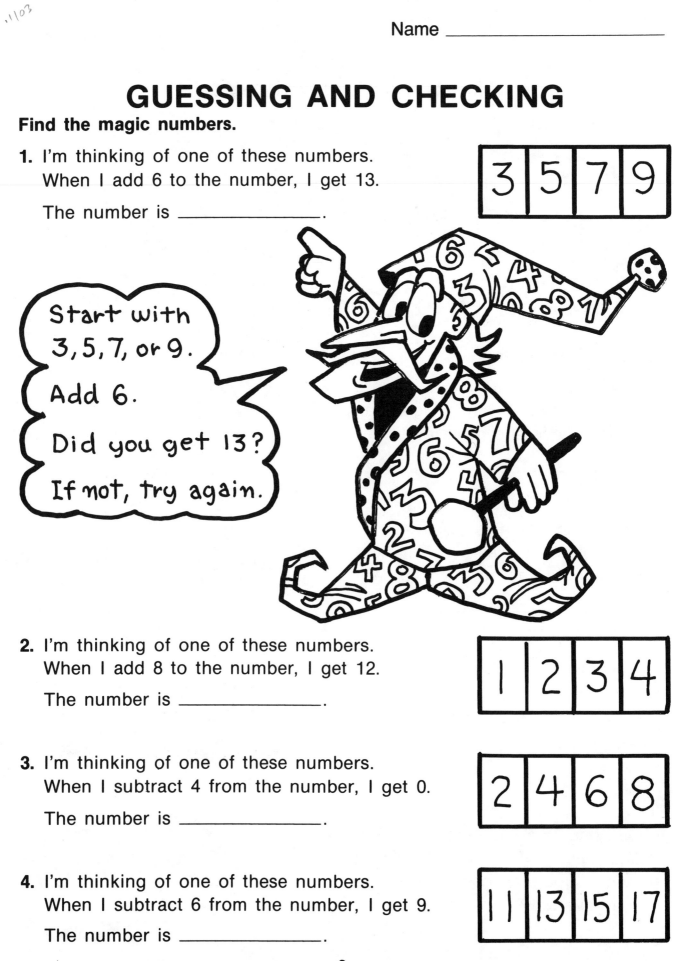

Name _____

GUESSING AND CHECKING

Find the magic numbers.

1. I'm thinking of one of these numbers.
   When I add 6 to the number, I get 13.

   The number is _____.

   | 3 | 5 | 7 | 9 |

   Start with 3, 5, 7, or 9.

   Add 6.

   Did you get 13?

   If not, try again.

2. I'm thinking of one of these numbers.
   When I add 8 to the number, I get 12.

   The number is _____.

   | 1 | 2 | 3 | 4 |

3. I'm thinking of one of these numbers.
   When I subtract 4 from the number, I get 0.

   The number is _____.

   | 2 | 4 | 6 | 8 |

4. I'm thinking of one of these numbers.
   When I subtract 6 from the number, I get 9.

   The number is _____.

   | 11 | 13 | 15 | 17 |

6

Name _____

SOLVING PROBLEMS

Solve each problem.

1. Pat saved $9. Mickey saved $15. How much more money did Mickey save than Pat?

_____

2. Carla bought 15 postage stamps. She used 6 stamps. How many stamps does she have left?

_____

3. Carla's mother bought 12 eggs. She used 5 eggs for the family breakfast. How many eggs does she have left?

_____

4. Arnie drew 11 pictures. Ben drew 6 pictures. How many more pictures did Arnie draw than Ben?

_____

SOLVING PROBLEMS

Solve each problem.

1. Spencer bought a truck for 8 cents. He also bought a car for 6 cents. How much did he spend in all?

   _____

2. Tiffany had 15 cents. She spent 6 cents for an airplane. How much did she have left?

   _____

3. Mannie had 7 cents. He made 5 cents by selling a book. Then how much money did he have?

   _____

4. Miriam took 20 cents to the sale. She spent 10 cents for a truck. How much did she have left?

   _____

8

FINDING FACTS IN A PICTURE

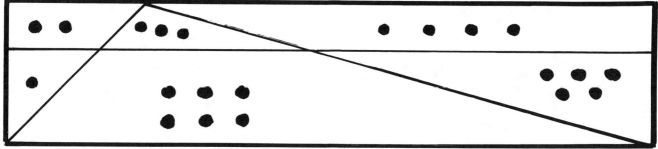

How many dots are in these pictures?

FIND THE FACTS

1. _____ dots

2. _____ dots

3. _____ dots

4. _____ dots

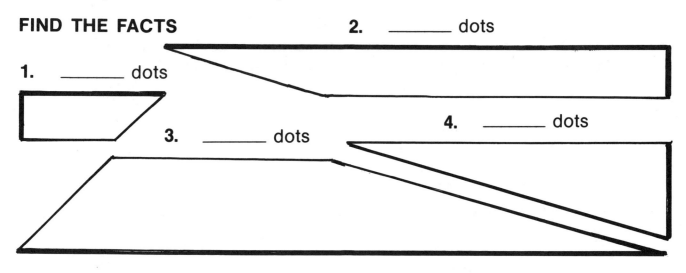

USE THE FACTS

5. _____ dots

6. _____ dots

7. _____ dots

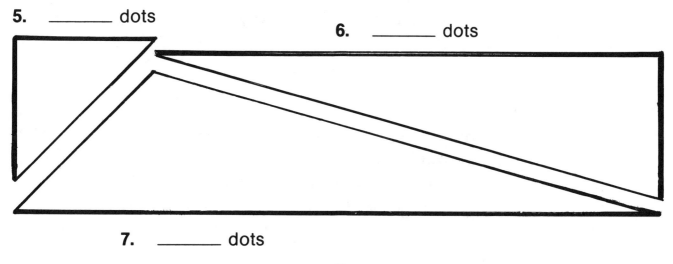

9

SOLVING PROBLEMS

Solve each problem.

1. Diane did 7 magic tricks at the party. Mario did 5 magic tricks at the party. How many magic tricks did they do in all?

_____

2. Mario had 14 magic cards. He made 6 cards vanish. How many cards were left?

_____

3. Diane did a trick with 15 ribbons. Six of the ribbons were red. The other ribbons were blue. How many blue ribbons were there?

_____

4. Linda juggled 3 plates with her left hand and 2 plates with her right hand. How many plates did she juggle altogether?

_____

FINDING FACTS IN A TABLE

Name	Number of Push-ups
Ruth	7
Booker	15
Pete	12
Maria	18

Find Pete. Look across to the number.

FIND THE FACTS

1. How many push-ups did Pete do? _____

2. Who did 15 push-ups? _____

Find 15. Look back to the name.

3. Who did 7 push-ups? _____

4. How many push-ups did Maria do? _____

USE THE FACTS

5. How many push-ups did Ruth and Pete do altogether? _____

6. How many more push-ups did Booker do than Pete? _____

7. How many fewer push-ups did Pete do than Maria? _____

8. How many push-ups did Booker and Pete do in all? _____

GUESSING AND CHECKING

Find the numbers.

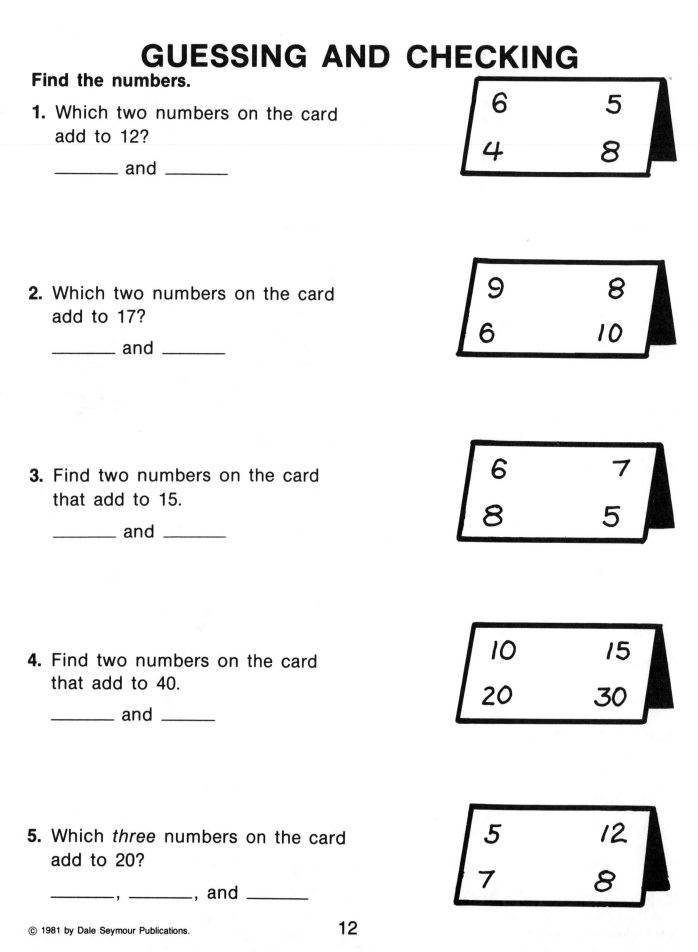

1. Which two numbers on the card add to 12?

_____ and _____

2. Which two numbers on the card add to 17?

_____ and _____

3. Find two numbers on the card that add to 15.

_____ and _____

4. Find two numbers on the card that add to 40.

_____ and _____

5. Which *three* numbers on the card add to 20?

_____, _____, and _____

FINDING FACTS IN A TABLE

Chris asked the students in his class, "What color do you like best?" He put their answers in a table.

Color	Number
red	6
blue	10
yellow	4
green	5
purple	2

Find yellow. Look across to the number.

FIND THE FACTS

1. How many students chose yellow? _____

2. How many students chose purple? _____

3. Which color was chosen 6 times? _____

Find 6. Look back to the color.

USE THE FACTS

4. Which color was chosen the greatest number of times? _____

5. How many more students chose red than purple? _____

6. How many fewer students chose green than blue? _____

7. How many students answered Chris' question? _____

FINDING FACTS IN A STORY

A FUNNY STORY

Mr. Rooter's refrigerator loved food. For 20 years the refrigerator kept all of the food fresh. One day the refrigerator ate 6 apples, 5 peaches, and 3 oranges. Then the refrigerator drank 1 quart of milk and 2 quarts of orange juice. When Mr. Rooter came home, he thought that the refrigerator looked full. But when he opened the door, it was empty!

FIND THE FACTS

1. How many apples did the refrigerator eat? _____

2. How many oranges did the refrigerator eat? _____

3. How many quarts of milk did the refrigerator

drink? _____

4. How many quarts of orange juice did the

refrigerator drink? _____

USE THE FACTS

5. How many more peaches did the refrigerator eat than

oranges? _____

6. How many apples, peaches, and oranges did the

refrigerator eat in all? _____

7. How many quarts of orange juice and milk did the

refrigerator drink altogether? _____

FINDING FACTS IN A CALENDAR

OCTOBER						
Sun.	Mon.	Tues.	Wed.	Thurs.	Fri.	Sat.
					1	2
3	4	5	6	7	8	9
10	11	12	13	14	15	16
17	18	19	20	21	22	23
24	25	26	27	28	29	30
31						

FIND THE FACTS

1. How many days are there in October? _____

Find Sunday. Look down and count the dates.

2. How many Sundays are there in October? _____

3. How many Mondays are there in October? _____

4. What is the date of the first Monday in October? _____

5. Halloween is October 31. What day of the week is Halloween? _____

6. October 11 is one week after October 4.

   October _____ is one week after October 5.

7. October 20 is one week before October 27.

   October _____ is one week before October 29.

15

FINDING FACTS IN A TABLE

Name	Number of Tickets Sold
Jenny	30
Lamar	25
Cliff	13
Rhonda	24
Becka	11
Scott	16

Find Lamar. Look across to the number.

FIND THE FACTS

1. How many tickets did Lamar sell? _____

2. How many tickets did Cliff sell? _____

3. Who sold 24 tickets? _____

4. Who sold 16 tickets? _____

Find 24. Look back to the name.

USE THE FACTS

5. Who sold the most tickets? _____

6. How many tickets did Jenny and Rhonda sell together? _____

7. Which two boys sold a total of 29 tickets?

_____ and _____

8. Which two girls sold a total of 41 tickets?

_____ and _____

FINDING FACTS IN A STORY

ARTURO'S BIRTHDAY PARTY

Arturo's birthday was November 12. He had a big party. Nine boys and 8 girls came to the party. Arturo gave a balloon to each of the children. Six of the balloons were red. All the other balloons were green. Arturo got lots of presents.

FIND THE FACTS

1. How many boys were at the party? _____

2. How many girls were at the party? _____

3. How many balloons were red? _____

USE THE FACTS

4. How many more boys than girls came to the party? _____

5. How many children came to the party altogether? _____

6. How many green balloons did Arturo give away? _____

© 1981 by Dale Seymour Publications.

17

FINDING FACTS ON A MAP

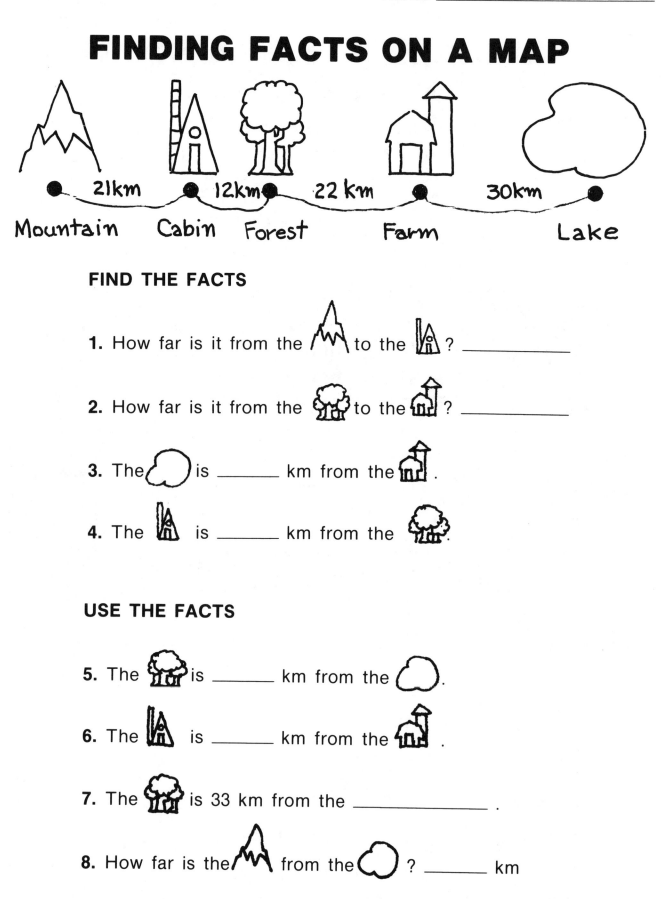

21km 12km 22 km 30km

Mountain   Cabin   Forest   Farm   Lake

FIND THE FACTS

1. How far is it from the ⛰ to the 🏠 ? _____

2. How far is it from the 🌳 to the 🏠 ? _____

3. The ☁ is _____ km from the 🏠 .

4. The 🏠 is _____ km from the 🌳 .

USE THE FACTS

5. The 🌳 is _____ km from the ☁ .

6. The 🏠 is _____ km from the 🏠 .

7. The 🌳 is 33 km from the _____ .

8. How far is the ⛰ from the ☁ ? _____ km

SOLVING PROBLEMS

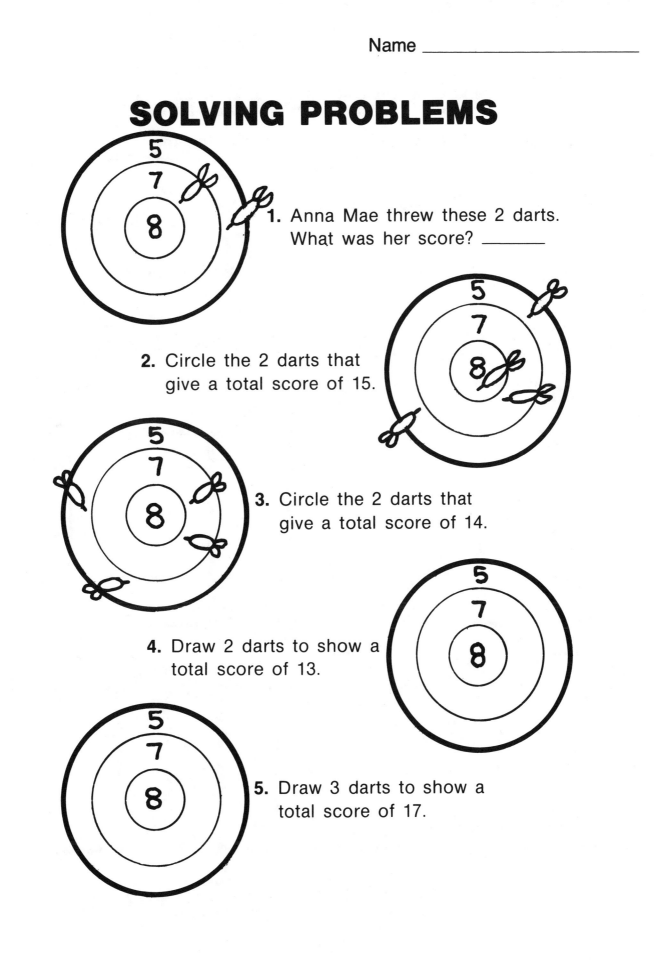

1. Anna Mae threw these 2 darts. What was her score? _____

2. Circle the 2 darts that give a total score of 15.

3. Circle the 2 darts that give a total score of 14.

4. Draw 2 darts to show a total score of 13.

5. Draw 3 darts to show a total score of 17.

MAKING DRAWINGS

At the pet shop, Ms. Domuch put goldfish into the tanks.

She put 4 goldfish into each large tank.

She put 2 goldfish into each small tank.

How many goldfish did she put into the tanks altogether?

Draw the fish in the tanks.

Count to find the answer.

There are _____ goldfish altogether.

SOLVING PROBLEMS

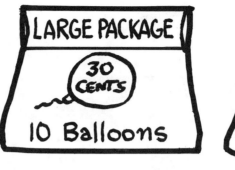

Solve each problem.

1. James bought a jumbo package and a large package of balloons. He spent a total of

   _____

2. Tina bought a jumbo package and a small package. How many balloons did she buy? _____

3. Martin bought a package of balloons. He used 6 of the balloons and had 14 left. What size package did Martin buy? _____

4. Billie bought 16 balloons. She bought a large package and a _____ package.

5. Jill spent 65 cents for balloons. She bought a jumbo package and a _____ package.

6. Doug spent 45 cents for balloons. He bought a total of _____ balloons.

FINDING FACTS IN A PICTURE

FIND THE FACTS

1. How much does the loaf of bread cost? _____

2. What is the price of the cheese? _____

3. Which food costs 69 cents? _____

USE THE FACTS

4. What is the total cost of a loaf of bread
and a jar of jam? _____

5. How much more does the cheese cost than
the jam? _____

6. Ms. Abruzzi bought a jar of jam.
She gave the clerk 75 cents.
How much change did she get?

_____

7. How much would you pay for a
loaf of bread with this coupon?

_____

10¢   **SAVE!**   10¢
10 cents OFF the price
1 loaf wheat bread.
10¢   10¢

USING LOGIC

1. Which hat belongs to Mrs. Flippity-Flop?

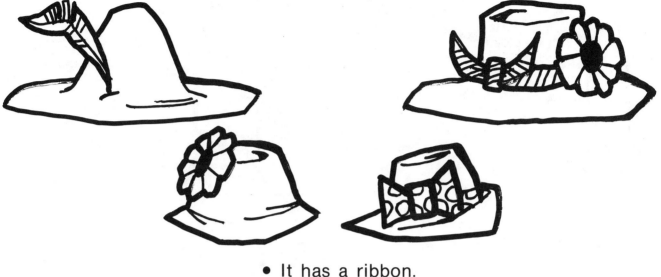

- It has a ribbon.
- It is *not* small.
- It has a flower.

Draw a ring around Mrs. Flippity-Flop's hat.

2. Which bow tie belongs to Mr. Hoppity-Hip?

- It has dots.
- It does *not* have stars.
- There is a frog in the middle of the tie.

Draw a ring around Mr. Hoppity-Hip's bow tie.

SOLVING PROBLEMS

Fish puzzle – 67 cents

1. How much more does a fish puzzle cost than a frog puzzle?

   _____

2. Robin bought a turtle puzzle. She gave the clerk 25 cents. How much change did Robin get?

   _____

3. Halona bought a fish puzzle. Sally bought a turtle puzzle. How much more did Halona spend than Sally?

   _____

4. Suppose you have 50 cents. Which puzzles could you buy?

   _____

   How much change would you get?

   _____

Frog puzzle – 45 cents

Turtle puzzle – 14 cents

SOLVING PROBLEMS

Name	Number of Jumps
Victor	35
Juana	57
Anita	23
Joey	51

1. How many more jumps did Juana make than Anita?

_____

2. How many fewer jumps did Victor make than Joey?

_____

3. How much more does the large box cost than the small box?

_____

4. How many more flies are in the large box than in the small box?

_____

25

GUESSING AND CHECKING

Solve each problem.

1. Put an X on the 2 coins that are worth 26 cents.

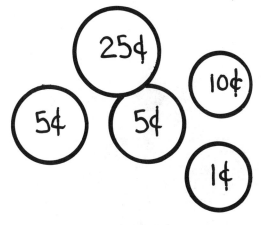

2. Put an X on the 2 coins that are worth 35 cents.

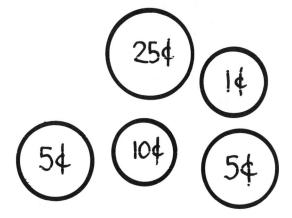

3. Put an X on the 3 coins that are worth 36 cents.

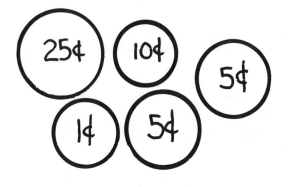

4. Put an X on the 3 coins that are worth 35 cents.

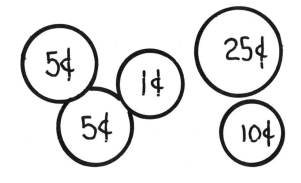

5. Put an X on the 3 coins that are worth 16 cents.

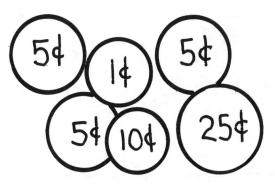

6. Put an X on the 4 coins that are worth 25 cents.

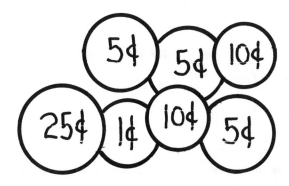

26

SOLVING PROBLEMS

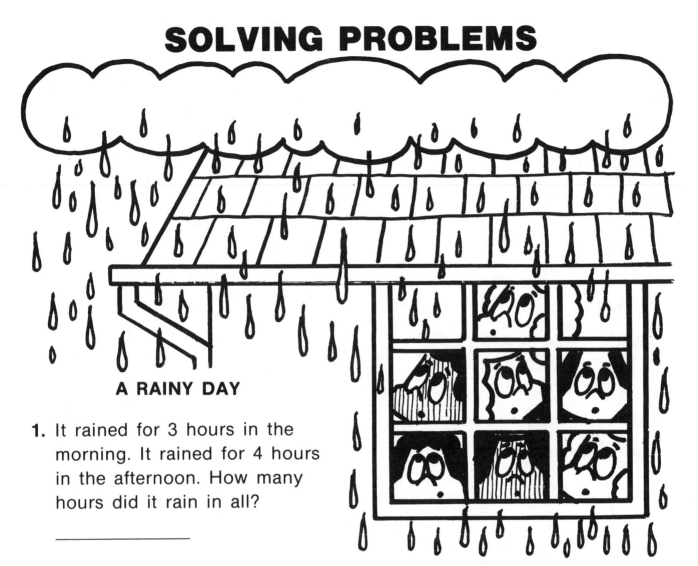

A RAINY DAY

1. It rained for 3 hours in the morning. It rained for 4 hours in the afternoon. How many hours did it rain in all?

   _____

2. Velma and Jan played checkers. Velma won 7 games. Jan won 9 games. How many more games did Jan win than Velma?

   _____

3. Bert read a book about horses. He read 34 pages before lunch. He read 25 pages after lunch. How many pages did Bert read altogether?

   _____

4. Clark practiced the piano for 45 minutes. Sandra practiced for 35 minutes. How much longer did Clark practice than Sandra?

   _____ minutes

5. Seth and Judy made paper airplanes. Seth made 23. Judy made 24. How many paper airplanes did they make in all?

   _____

27

FINDING FACTS IN A LIST

Teacher	Number of Students
Mrs. Alvarez	28
Mr. Brook	30
Mr. Chao	26
Mrs. Doyle	27
Mr. Edwards	31

Find Mr. Chao. Look across to the number.

Find 27. Look back to the name.

FIND THE FACTS

1. How many students are there in Mr. Chao's class? _____

2. How many students are there in Mrs. Alvarez's class? _____

3. Which teacher has 27 students? _____

4. Which teacher has 30 students? _____

USE THE FACTS

5. Which teacher has the greatest number of students? _____

6. How many students are there in Mr. Brook's and Mrs. Doyle's classes altogether? _____

7. How many more students are there in Mr. Edward's class than in Mr. Chao's class? _____

8. Mrs. Alvarez has 13 girls in her class. How many boys are there in her class? _____

FINDING FACTS IN A LIST

Find the fact you need to solve the problem. Then solve the problem.

1. Joni made some muffins. She ate 2 of them. How many muffins did she have left?

   _____

2. The library opens in the morning and closes at 5:00 in the afternoon. How many hours is the library open in one day?

   _____

3. Matt bought a book for $3.00. Later, he bought a race car. How much money did Matt spend altogether?

   _____

4. Ms. Wilson ran 5 kilometers on Monday. She also ran on Tuesday. How many kilometers did she run in all?

   _____

5. On Monday, the flower store sold some roses. The store also sold 30 mums. How many more roses were sold than mums?

   _____

FACT LIST

- The race car cost $2.00.
- The library opens at 9:00 in the morning.
- The flower store sold 100 roses.
- Joni made 10 muffins.
- Ms. Wilson ran 7 kilometers on Tuesday.

SOLVING PROBLEMS

Mario has a job feeding animals.

1. This morning, Mario fed 34 large dogs. He fed 22 small dogs. How many dogs did he feed in all?

   _____

2. There were 29 hungry cats. Mario fed 23 of the cats. How many cats are left to feed?

   _____

3. The pet store had 85 bags of dog food. It used 62 bags. How many bags does it have left?

   _____

4. There were 68 bones. Mario gave one bone to each of the 56 dogs. How many bones were left?

   _____

5. Last week Mario earned $12. This week he earned $17. How much money did he earn altogether?

   _____

GUESSING AND CHECKING

RADIO $7.00

FOOTBALL $3.00

CAMERA $12.00

HELMET $9.00

1. Which two items cost a total of $12? Circle your answer.

helmet and football

radio and camera

2. Which two items cost a total of $15? Circle your answer.

football and helmet

camera and football

radio and helmet

Make your own guesses to solve these problems.

3. Which two items cost a total of $19? _____ and _____

4. Which two items cost a total of $10? _____ and _____

5. Which two items cost a total of $16? _____ and _____

6. Which three items cost a total of $19?

_____ , _____ , and _____ .

FINDING FACTS IN A CALENDAR

J U L Y						
Sun.	Mon.	Tues.	Wed.	Thurs.	Fri.	Sat.
		1	2	3	4	5
6	7	8	9	10	11	12
13	14	15	16	17	18	19
20	21	22	23	24	25	26
27	28	29	30	31		

Find the number 8. Look up to find the name of the day.

1. On what day of the week is July 8? _____

2. On what day of the week is July 4? _____

Find Monday. Look down. Count the dates.

3. How many Mondays are there in this month? _____

4. How many Thursdays are there in this month? _____

5. On July 7, Lynette took out a library book.
The librarian told her to bring the book back
on Wednesday. On what date was the book due?

_____

6. On what day of the week is August 1? _____

32

FINDING FACTS IN A PICTURE

Number of Tinker Toy pieces

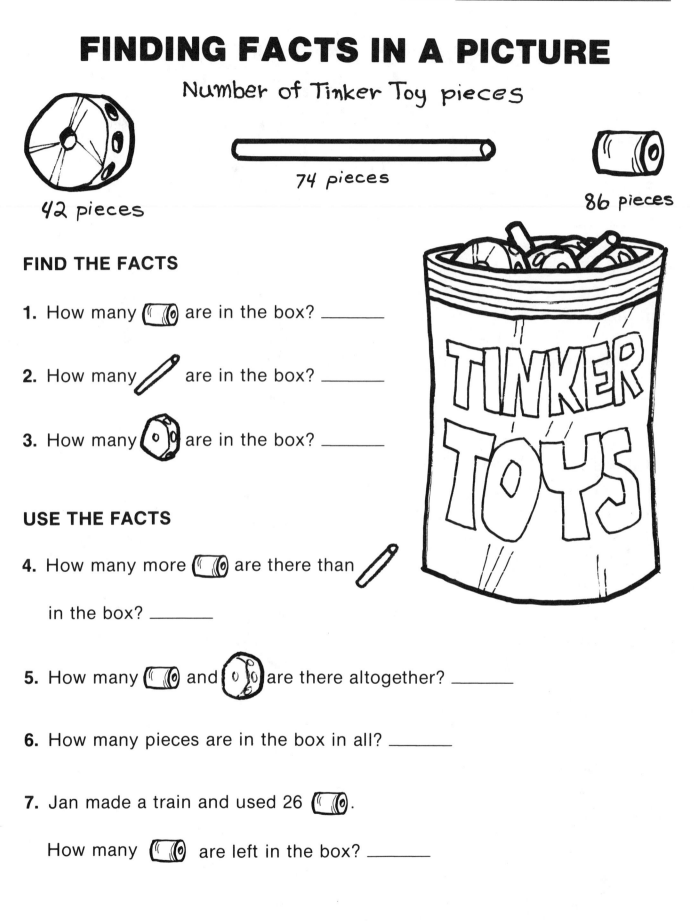

42 pieces

74 pieces

86 pieces

FIND THE FACTS

1. How many are in the box? _____

2. How many are in the box? _____

3. How many are in the box? _____

USE THE FACTS

4. How many more are there than

in the box? _____

5. How many and are there altogether? _____

6. How many pieces are in the box in all? _____

7. Jan made a train and used 26 .

How many are left in the box? _____

33

SOLVING PROBLEMS

1. Miss Croft bought a bird feeder for $12. She bought some bird food for $4. What was the total cost?

_____

2. There are 140 paper napkins in the large package. There are 65 napkins in the small package. How many more napkins are there in the large package than in the small package?

_____

3. The park is 25 kilometers from Kathy's house. The lake is 42 kilometers from Kathy's house. How many more kilometers is the lake than the park from Kathy's house?

_____ km

4. Jones read for 20 minutes before supper. He read for 35 minutes after supper. How many minutes did Jones read in all?

_____

5. The radio costs $45. The clock costs $37. How much more does the radio cost than the clock?

_____

FINDING FACTS IN A TABLE

SCORE ON TURN 1	
Lisa	5
Nick	7
Leo	10
Sandy	2
Judy	0

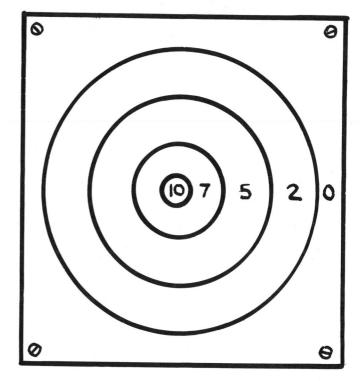

FIND THE FACTS

1. What was Lisa's score on her first turn? _____

2. What was Sandy's score on his first turn? _____

3. Who scored 10 on the first turn? _____

USE THE FACTS

4. Who had the highest score on the first turn? _____

5. Nick scored 5 points on his second turn. What was Nick's total score for the two turns? _____

6. After Sandy's second turn, his total score was 9. How many points did Sandy score on his second turn? _____

7. Judy had a total of 10 points after her second turn. How many points did she score on her second turn? _____

SOLVING PROBLEMS

1. Cindy had 95¢. She bought a sticker for 19¢. How much money does she have left?

_____

2. Dale sold 22 tickets for the school play. Margo sold 17 tickets for the play. How many fewer tickets did Margo sell than Dale?

_____

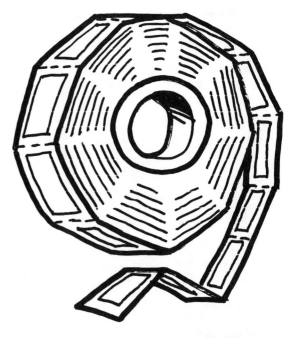

3. Donna sold 23 tickets on Saturday. She sold 15 tickets on Sunday. How many tickets did she sell in all?

_____

4. Terry is 6 years old. Patty is 9 years older than Terry. How old is Patty?

_____

5. Carlos is 132 centimeters tall. His father is 158 centimeters tall. How much taller is Carlos' father?

_____

MAKING DRAWINGS

How many worms does Danny have?

Danny had 4 bags of worms.

There are 5 worms in bag A.

There are the same number of worms in bag B as in bag A.

There are 3 more worms in bag C than in bag A.

There are 2 worms in bag D.

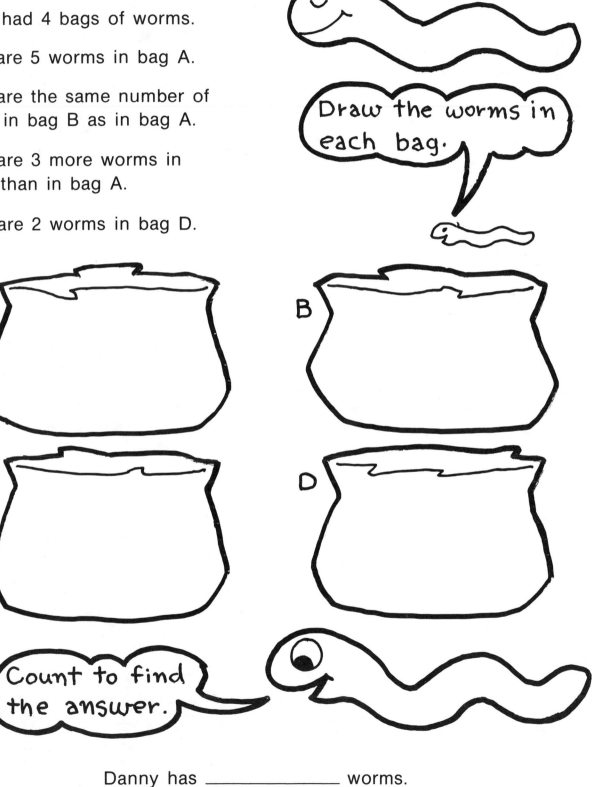

Draw the worms in each bag.

A

B

C

D

Count to find the answer.

Danny has _____ worms.

SOLVING PROBLEMS

1. Susan went to the Flower Show. She saw 26 red roses and 17 white roses. How many roses did she see altogether?

   _____

2. The large box of rice weighs 950 grams. The small box of rice weighs 510 grams. How much more does the large box weigh than the small box?

   _____ gm

3. Tony had 54 comic books. He gave 8 of them to Fred. How many comic books does Tony have left?

   _____

   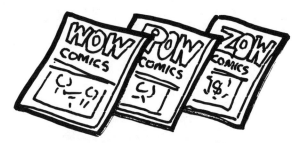

4. Jerry collected 23 empty bottles. Neal collected 19 empty bottles. How many bottles did they collect altogether?

   _____

5. Dan is 14 years old. Joel is 6 years younger than Dan. How old is Joel?

   _____

FINDING FACTS IN A PICTURE

10¢

5¢   5¢

Amy's Coins

10¢

25¢

Bill's Coins

10¢   10¢

10¢   10¢

Ted's Coins

5¢

25¢   25¢

Kari's Coins

FIND THE FACTS

1. Who has 40 cents? _____

2. How much money does Amy have? _____ ¢

3. Who has 55 cents? _____

4. How much money does Bill have? _____ ¢

USE THE FACTS

5. Who has 15 cents more than Ted? _____

6. Who has more money, Bill or Amy? _____

How much more? _____ ¢

7. Do Bill and Ted have enough money altogether

to buy a kite for 69¢? _____

GUESSING AND CHECKING

RIDES	
Ghost Train	3 tickets
Bumper Cars	4 tickets
Rocket Ship	8 tickets
Roller Coaster	10 tickets

1. Nancy went on two different rides.
She used 12 tickets.
What were the rides?

Speech bubbles: "Guess two rides." / "Add the number of tickets for each ride." / "Did you get 12? If not, guess again."

Nancy went on the _____ and the _____ .

2. Hali went on two different rides.
She used 18 tickets.

Hali went on the _____ and the _____ .

3. Larry went on two different rides.
He used 13 tickets.

Larry went on the _____ and the _____ .

4. Stan went on three different rides.
He used 17 tickets.

Stan went on the _____, _____, and the _____ .

SOLVING PROBLEMS

1. Peter bought 3 boxes of Purr Cat Food. How many cans of cat food did he buy altogether?

_____

2. There are 8 small boxes of cereal in each pack. Miss Benton bought 6 packs of cereal. How many boxes of of cereal did she buy in all?

_____

3. There are 8 oranges in each bag. How many oranges are there in 5 bags?

_____

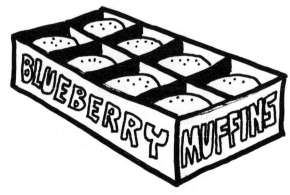

4. Mr. Carlton bought 3 packages of these muffins. How many muffins did he buy altogether?

_____

FINDING FACTS IN A SIGN

SPORT SHOP SALE Save on these items.	
Baseball	Now $2
Bat	Now $8
Glove	Now $12

FIND THE FACTS

1. How much does a bat cost on

   sale? _____

2. What is the price of a glove

   on sale? _____

USE THE FACTS

3. Mary Ann has $5. How much more
   does she need to buy a bat? _____

4. The regular price of a glove is $17.
   How much do you save by buying the
   glove on sale? _____

5. Mr. Simon bought 3 bats.
   What was the total cost of the bats? _____
   Mr. Simon gave the clerk $30.
   How much change did he get? _____

6. Berta bought 2 items on sale. She paid $14.
   What did Berta buy?

   _____ and _____

Make a guess.
Check your guess.

42

Name _____

USING LOGIC

Use the clues. Match the price tags to the items.

1. Clues
- The ball costs $2.
- The glove costs more than the bat.

$2
$5
$7

2. Clues
- The scissors cost 70 cents.
- The pen costs more than the ruler.

10¢
20¢
70¢

3. Clues
- The watch costs $8.
- Together the watch and book cost $10.

$2
$8
$9

4. Clues
- Together the car and boat cost $9.
- The car costs $5.

$2
$4
$5

43

FINDING FACTS IN A STORY

KEEPING FIT

The children in Mrs. Kelly's class did exercises every morning. Pedro did 96 jumping jacks. Jerry did 40 jumping jacks. Debbie did 55 jumping jacks. Richard did 24 sit-ups. Bob touched his toes 40 **times**. Mrs. Kelly touched her toes 50 **times**.

FIND THE FACTS

1. Pedro did _____ jumping jacks.

2. Jerry did _____ jumping jacks.

3. How many times did Bob touch his toes? _____

4. How many times did Mrs. Kelly touch her toes? _____

USE THE FACTS

5. How many more jumping jacks did Pedro do than Jerry? _____

6. How many jumping jacks did Jerry and Debbie do altogether? _____

7. How many jumping jacks did the three children do in all? _____

8. How many more times did Mrs. Kelly touch her toes than Bob touched his toes? _____

SOLVING PROBLEMS

TICKET PRICES	
Adult	$4
Child	$2

LITTLE WORLD SERIES
9 BIG GAMES
GET YOUR TICKETS NOW!

Find the price of a child's ticket. Multiply to find the total cost.

1. How much do 5 children's tickets cost?

_____

2. Mr. Costa bought 7 adult tickets. How much did he pay in all?

_____

3. Slugger Judy batted 3 times in each of the 9 games. How many times did Slugger Judy bat in all?

_____

4. Mrs. Barnes bought one adult ticket and some children's tickets. She paid $14. How many children's tickets did she buy?

_____

GUESSING AND CHECKING

**Pick a card. Do the numbers fit the facts?
If not, pick another card.**

1. Facts
- When you add the numbers you get 11.
- When you subtract the numbers you get 3.

The numbers are _____ and _____ .

8,4	7,4
6,3	9,2

2. Facts
- When you multiply the numbers you get 24.
- When you add the numbers you get 10.

The numbers are _____ and _____ .

8,3	2,12
1,9	6,4

3. Facts
- The sum of the numbers is 24.
- The difference of the numbers is 4.

The numbers are _____ and _____ .

8,4	6,4
14,10	13,11

4. Facts
- The product of the numbers is 36.
- The difference of the numbers is 5.

The numbers are _____ and _____ .

6,6	12,3
12,7	9,4

SOLVING PROBLEMS

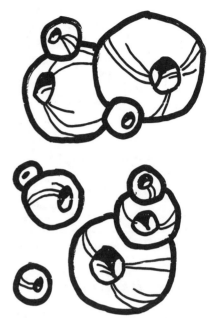

BEADS	
Small	2¢
Medium	4¢
Large	6¢

1. What is the cost of 6 small
   beads? _____

2. Mara bought 9 large beads.
   What was the total cost of the
   beads? _____

3. Manny made 4 rings.
   Each ring had 5 beads.
   How many beads did Manny use? _____

4. What size beads did Carmen buy? _____
   Clues
   • All of the beads were the same size.
   • She paid 16¢ for the beads.
   • She bought more than 5 beads.

Make a guess.
Check your guess.

5. How many beads did Patsy buy? _____
   Clues
   • All of the beads were the same size.
   • She paid 24¢ for the beads.
   • She bought fewer than 5 beads.

47

FINDING FACTS ON A MAP

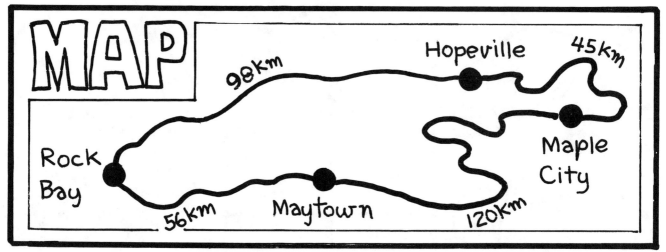

FIND THE FACTS

1. How many kilometers is it from Rock Bay
to Maytown? _____

2. How many kilometers is it from Rock Bay
to Hopeville? _____

3. Which city is 120 kilometers from Maple City? _____

4. Which city is 45 kilometers from Maple City? _____

USE THE FACTS

5. How many more kilometers is it from Rock Bay
to Hopeville than from Rock Bay to Maytown? _____

6. Jane went from Maytown to Maple City to Hopeville.
How many kilometers did Jane travel in all? _____

7. Ron is going from Maytown to Maple City. He has
already gone 50 kilometers. How many kilometers
does he have left to go? _____

SOLVING PROBLEMS

NEWS

1. Mark has a newspaper route. He delivers 50 Sunday papers and 35 daily papers. How many more Sunday papers does he deliver than daily papers?

_____

NEWS

2. A Sunday paper costs 75¢. A daily paper costs 25¢. How much less does a daily paper cost than a Sunday paper?

_____

NEWS

3. There were 45 pages in Friday's paper. Mark's father has read 36 pages. How many pages does he have left to read?

_____

NEWS

4. There were two special magazines in Sunday's paper. One magazine was 26 pages long. The other magazine was 38 pages long. How many magazine pages were there in all?

_____

49

GUESSING AND CHECKING

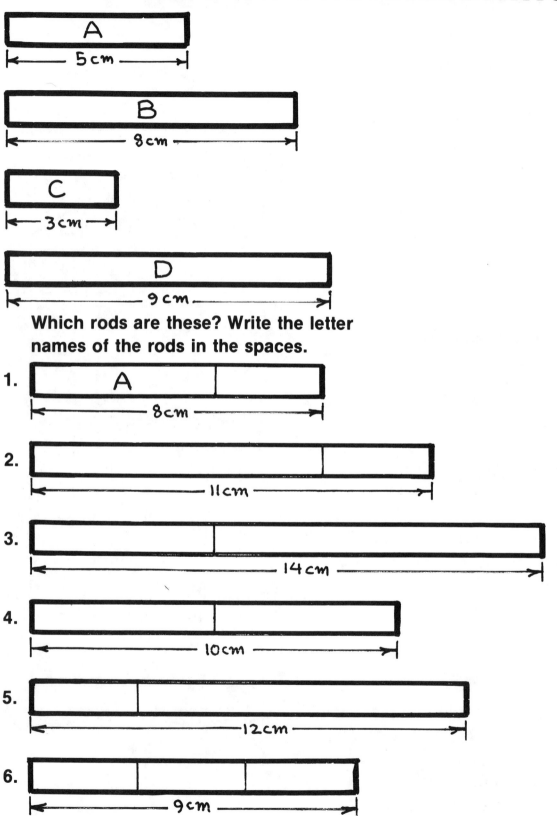

A — 5cm

B — 8cm

C — 3cm

D — 9cm

Which rods are these? Write the letter names of the rods in the spaces.

1. A — 8cm

2. — 11cm

3. — 14cm

4. — 10cm

5. — 12cm

6. — 9cm

FINDING FACTS IN A STORY

MYSTERY ISLAND

Betty made up a story about a place called Mystery Island. Betty was lost on the Island. She met 5 cats and 6 dogs. She needed to make a shelter. She used 100 oak branches and 25 pine branches. She had to walk 2 kilometers each day to get fresh water. Every night she heard strange noises. She was very glad when a ship captain found her. 2 of the cats and 1 dog decided to go home with her.

Bye, bye.

FIND THE FACTS

1. How many cats did Betty meet on the Island? _____

2. How many pine branches did Betty use for her shelter? _____

3. How many kilometers did she have to walk to get fresh water each day? _____

4. How many cats decided to go home with her? _____

USE THE FACTS

5. How many animals did Betty meet on the Island in all? _____

6. Betty went to get water 4 times. How many kilometers did she walk altogether? _____

7. Altogether, how many branches did Betty use for her shelter? _____

8. How many of the dogs did *not* go home with Betty? _____

51

FINDING FACTS IN A SIGN

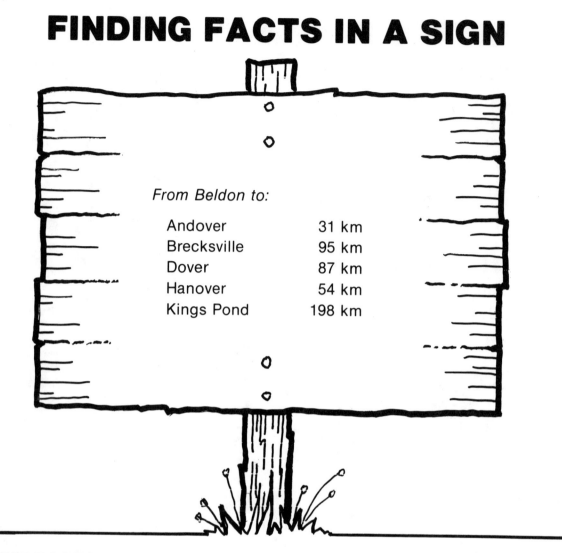

From Beldon to:

Andover	31 km
Brecksville	95 km
Dover	87 km
Hanover	54 km
Kings Pond	198 km

FIND THE FACTS

1. The distance from Beldon to Andover is _____ km.

2. The distance from Beldon to Hanover is _____ km.

3. The distance from Beldon to _____ is 87 km.

4. The distance from Beldon to _____ is 198 km.

USE THE FACTS

5. Which city is closest to Beldon? _____

6. Which city is farthest from Beldon? _____

7. How much farther is Brecksville than Hanover? _____

8. How much farther is Dover than Andover? _____

Name _____

SOLVING PROBLEMS

1. Ms. Grange bought 4 packages of light bulbs. How many bulbs did she buy?

   _____

2. Mr. Ward bought 5 packages of tomatoes. How many tomatoes did he buy in all?

   _____

3. Ted bought 3 packs of baseball cards. How many cards did he buy altogether?

   _____

4. Jessie bought 6 packs of pencils. How many pencils did she buy in all?

   _____

SOLVING PROBLEMS

1. The garden store had a special sale. Ms. Jordan bought 3 small spider plants for $2 each. How much did she spend in all?

   _____

2. Mr. Grimes spent a total of $21 for pots. He bought 3 pots. Each pot cost the same amount. How much did each pot cost?

   _____

3. There were 5 rows of pansies. There were 8 boxes of pansies in each row. How many boxes of pansies were there altogether?

   _____

4. The store sells small lettuce plants in packs of 4. Joe wants 12 lettuce plants. How many packs of lettuce plants should he buy?

   _____

5. Outside the store there were 4 pretty window boxes. In each box, there were 5 plants. How many plants were there in the window boxes altogether?

   _____

FINDING FACTS IN A STORY

KITE FLYING

Saturday was a windy and sunny day. Kevin and Will bought a kite. The kite was 75 centimeters long. The tail of the kite was 200 centimeters long. There were 7 blue ribbons and 8 red ribbons on the tail.

Kevin flew the kite for 12 minutes. Will flew the kite for 15 minutes. Then the kite got stuck in a tree.

FIND THE FACTS

1. How long was the kite? _____ centimeters

2. How long was the tail of the kite? _____ centimeters

3. How many red ribbons were on the tail? _____

4. How many minutes did Kevin fly the kite? _____

USE THE FACTS

5. How many centimeters longer was the tail

of the kite than the kite? _____ centimeters

6. How many minutes did the boys fly the kite altogether?

_____

7. How many colored ribbons were on the tail of the kite?

_____

8. How many more minutes did Will fly the kite than Kevin?

_____

55

FINDING FACTS IN A SIGN

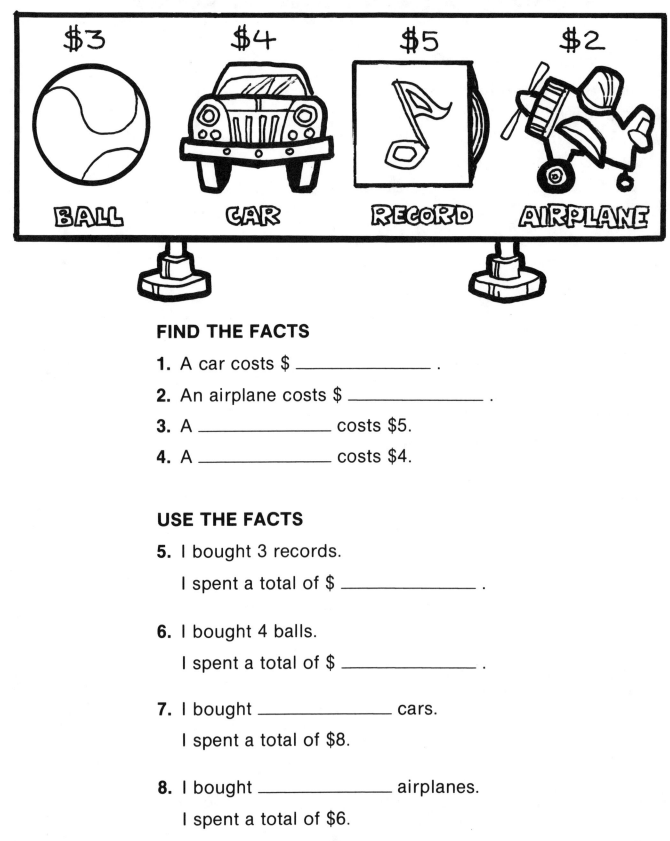

$3 BALL

$4 CAR

$5 RECORD

$2 AIRPLANE

FIND THE FACTS

1. A car costs $ _____ .

2. An airplane costs $ _____ .

3. A _____ costs $5.

4. A _____ costs $4.

USE THE FACTS

5. I bought 3 records.

I spent a total of $ _____ .

6. I bought 4 balls.

I spent a total of $ _____ .

7. I bought _____ cars.

I spent a total of $8.

8. I bought _____ airplanes.

I spent a total of $6.

USING DRAWINGS

1. Mr. Birch planted 4 rows of trees. There were 5 trees in each row. How many trees did Mr. Birch plant altogether?

_____

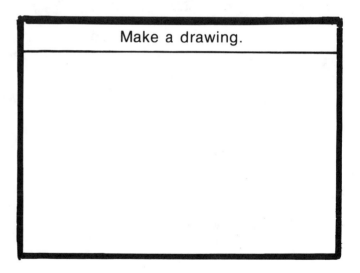

Make a drawing.

2. In the mini-forest, there is 1 row of 5 trees. There are also 2 rows with 3 trees in each row. How many trees are there in the mini-forest?

_____

Make a drawing.

3. You want to plant 1 tree in the first row, 2 trees in the second row, 3 trees in the third row, and 4 trees in the fourth row. How many trees will you need in all?

_____

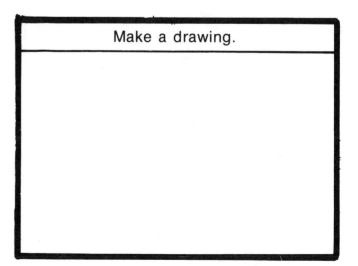

Make a drawing.

Name _____

FINDING FACTS IN A STORY

Jim and Paul weeded 3 flower beds. They were paid $2 for each flower bed. They also weeded 4 gardens. They were paid $3 for each garden. They earned a total of $18.

FIND THE FACTS

1. How many flower beds did the boys weed? _____

2. How much money were they paid for each flower bed? _____

3. How many gardens did they weed? _____

4. How much were they paid for each garden? _____

5. How much did they earn in all? _____

USE THE FACTS

6. Altogether, how much money were they paid for

   weeding the flower beds? _____

7. How much were they paid in all for weeding

   the gardens? _____

8. The boys shared the money they earned. They each got the

   same amount. How much money did each boy get? _____

GUESSING AND CHECKING

Draw a line so that the numbers on each
side of the line add to the *sum.*

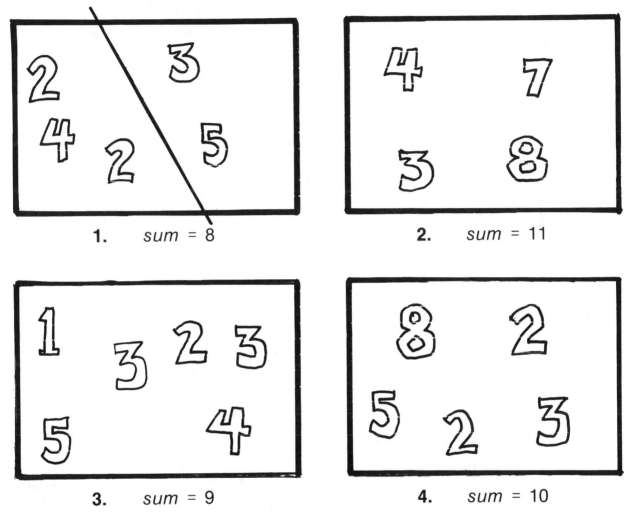

1.　　*sum = 8*

2.　　*sum = 11*

3.　　*sum = 9*

4.　　*sum = 10*

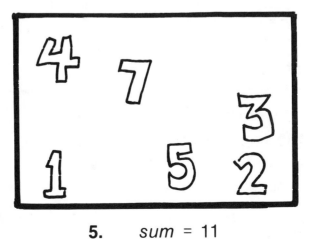

5.　　*sum = 11*

59

Name _____

SOLVING PROBLEMS

1. The Laughing Lions scored 18 points. Each of the 6 players scored the same number of points. How many points did each player score?

_____

2. The book cost $10. Barbara and Ken shared the cost equally. How much did Barbara pay?

_____

3. Mrs. Carter made 32 muffins. She put 8 muffins on each pan. How many pans did she use?

_____

4. David earned money raking leaves. He was paid $1 each hour. Yesterday he earned $6. How many hours did David work?

_____

5. Mary had a stamp book. On one page there were 40 stamps. There were 5 rows. There were the same number stamps in each row. How many stamps were in each row?

_____

60

USING LOGIC

Use the Clues. Match the price tags to the items.

1. Clues

- The apple costs 15¢.

- The pear costs more than the banana.

10¢   15¢   20¢

---

2. Clues

- The pen costs more than the pencil.

- The eraser costs 25¢.

20¢   25¢   99¢

---

3. Clues

- Together, the book and the puzzle cost $5.

- The book costs the most.

$1 $2 $3

---

4. Clues

- The dog collar costs $3 more than the bone.

$1 $3 $4

SOLVING PROBLEMS

1. The bakery sells fresh muffins in packages of 6. The package costs 60¢. How much does each muffin cost?

   _____

2. Judy bought 8 rolls. Each roll cost 9¢. How much did the rolls cost in all?

   _____

3. The baker makes raisin bread each day. Two cups of flour are needed for each loaf. How much flour is needed for 7 loaves?

   _____

4. The bakery has 3 shelves of pies. There are 4 pies on each shelf. How many pies are there altogether?

   _____

5. Joshua bought 36 fig bars. He asked the baker to put 6 fig bars in each box. How many boxes of fig bars did Joshua buy?

   _____

Name _____

FINDING FACTS IN A PICTURE

BAKE SALE

Muffins

60¢ total

Cookies

70¢ total

Brownies

45¢ total

Bread

$2 total

FIND THE FACTS

1. What is the cost of 6 muffins? _____

2. What is the cost of 5 brownies? _____

3. How many loaves of bread can you buy for $2? _____

4. How many cookies can you buy for 70¢? _____

USE THE FACTS

5. How much does 1 muffin cost? _____

6. What is the cost of 1 cookie? _____

7. What is the cost of 1 loaf of bread? _____

8. What is the cost of 3 loaves of bread? _____

63

Name _____

SOLVING PROBLEMS

The Brown family has a vegetable garden.

1. There are 20 pepper plants. There are 5 plants in each row. How many rows of pepper plants are there?

_____

2. Joey picked 12 tomatoes altogether. He picked the tomatoes from 3 plants. He picked the same number of tomatoes from each plant. How many tomatoes did he pick from each plant?

_____

3. The garden has 16 rows of plants. Carl weeds 2 rows of the garden each day. How many days does it take Carl to weed the garden?

_____

4. Marsha planted 18 squash seeds. She planted 3 seeds in each hill. How many hills of squash seeds did she plant?

_____

ANSWERS

page 1
1. 6
2. 9
3. 3, 2 (Numbers may be interchanged.)
4. 3

page 2
10 sails; student art should show 4 large boats with 2 sails each and 2 small bats with 1 sail each

page 3
1. 5 cups
2. 18 blueberries
3. 14 pancakes
4. 9 pancakes
5. 8 pancakes

page 4
Student art should show a circle around Damon, a box around Akito, and both a circle and a box around Esther.
1. Esther
2. the car

page 5
1. 6 posters
2. 4 glasses
3. 7 people
4. 4 Superman comic books

page 6
1. 7
2. 4
3. 4
4. 15

page 7
1. $6
2. 9 stamps
3. 7 eggs
4. 5 pictures

page 8
1. 14¢
2. 9¢
3. 12¢
4. 10¢

page 9
1. 2
2. 4
3. 6
4. 5
5. 3
6. 9
7. 9

page 10
1. 12 magic tricks
2. 8 cards
3. 9 blue ribbons
4. 5 plates

page 11
1. 12
2. Booker
3. Ruth
4. 18
5. 19
6. 3
7. 6
8. 27

page 12
1. 4 and 8
2. 9 and 8
3. 8 and 7
4. 10 and 30
5. 5, 7, and 8

page 13
1. 4
2. 2
3. red
4. blue
5. 4
6. 5
7. 27

page 14
1. 6
2. 3
3. 1 quart
4. 2 quarts
5. 2
6. 14
7. 3 quarts

page 15
1. 31
2. 5
3. 4
4. 4
5. Sunday
6. 12
7. 22

page 16
1. 25
2. 13
3. Rhonda
4. Scott
5. Jenny
6. 54
7. Scott and Cliff
8. Jenny and Becka

page 17
1. 9
2. 8
3. 6
4. 1
5. 17
6. 11

page 18
1. 21 km
2. 22 km
3. 30
4. 12
5. 52
6. 34
7. Student art should show a mountain.
8. 85

page 19
1. 12
2. The darts in the 8 section and the 7 ring should be circled.
3. The darts in the 7 ring should be circled.
4. There should be a dart in the 5 ring and in the 8 section.
5. There should be 2 darts in the 5 ring and 1 dart in the 7 ring.

page 20
Student art should show 4 goldfish in each large tank and 2 goldfish in each small tank; 14 goldfish altogether.

page 21
1. 80
2. 26
3. jumbo
4. small
5. small
6. 16

page 22
1. 50¢
2. 89¢
3. jam
4. $1.19
5. 20¢
6. 6¢
7. 40¢

page 23
1. The top-right hat should be circled.
2. The bottom-right bow tie should be circled.

page 24
1. 22¢
2. 11¢
3. 53¢
4. turtle or frog, 36¢ or 5¢

page 25
1. 34 jumps
2. 16 jumps
3. $1.23
4. 550 flies

page 26
1. 25¢, 1¢
2. 25¢, 10¢
3. 25¢, 10¢, 1¢
4. 25¢, 5¢, 5¢
5. 10¢, 5¢, 1¢ (any 5¢ piece)
6. 10¢, 5¢, 5¢, 5¢ (either 10¢ piece)

page 27
1. 7 hours
2. 2 games
3. 59 pages
4. 10 minutes
5. 47 paper airplanes

page 28
1. 26
2. 28
3. Mrs. Doyle
4. Mr. Brook
5. Mr. Edwards
6. 57 students
7. 5 students
8. 15 boys

page 29
1. 8 muffins
2. 8 hours
3. $5.00
4. 12 kilometers
5. 70 roses

page 30
1. 56 dogs
2. 6 cats
3. 23 bags
4. 12 bones
5. $29

page 31
1. helmet and football
2. camera and football
3. radio and camera
4. radio and football
5. radio and helmet
6. radio, football, and helmet

page 32
1. Tuesday
2. Friday
3. 4
4. 5
5. July 9
6. Friday

page 33
1. 86
2. 74
3. 42
4. 12
5. 128
6. 202
7. 60

page 34
1. $16
2. 75 napkins
3. 17 km
4. 55 minutes
5. $8

page 35
1. 5
2. 2
3. Leo
4. Leo
5. 12
6. 7
7. 10

page 36
1. 76¢
2. 5 tickets
3. 38 tickets
4. 15 years old
5. 26 centimeters

page 37
20 worms; student art should show 5 worms in Bag A, 5 worms in Bag B, 8 worms in Bag C, and 2 worms in Bag D

page 38
1. 43 roses
2. 440
3. 46 comic books
4. 42 bottles
5. 8 years old

page 39
1. Ted
2. 20¢
3. Kari
4. 35¢
5. Kari
6. Bill, 15¢
7. yes

page 40
1. bumper cars, rocket ship
2. rocket ship, roller coaster
3. ghost train, roller coaster
4. ghost train, bumper cars, roller coaster

page 41
1. 12 cans
2. 48 boxes
3. 40 oranges
4. 24 muffins

page 42
1. $8
2. $12
3. $3
4. $5
5. $24, $6
6. baseball, glove

page 43
1. glove $7, bat $5
2. pen 20¢, ruler 10¢, scissors 70¢
3. book $2, telescope $9, watch $8
4. boat $4, airplane $2, car $5

page 44
1. 96
2. 40
3. 40
4. 50
5. 56 jumping jacks
6. 95 jumping jacks
7. 191 jumping jacks
8. 10 times

page 45
1. $10
2. $28
3. 27 times
4. 5 children's tickets

page 46
1. 7 and 4
2. 6 and 4
3. 14 and 10
4. 9 and 4

page 47
1. 12¢
2. 54¢
3. 20 beads
4. small
5. 4 (large)

page 48
1. 56 km
2. 98 km
3. Maytown
4. Hopeville
5. 42 km
6. 165 km
7. 70 km

page 49
1. 15
2. 50¢
3. 9 pages
4. 64 pages

page 50
Letter names should be written on rods. The answers are given in order from left to right.
1. C
2. B, C
3. A, D
4. A, A
5. C, D
6. C, C, C

page 51
1. 5
2. 25
3. 2 km
4. 2
5. 11 animals
6. 8 km
7. 125 branches
8. 5 dogs

page 52

1. 31
2. 54
3. Dover
4. Kings Pond
5. Andover
6. Kings Pond
7. 41 km
8. 56 km

page 53

1. 8 bulbs
2. 15 tomatoes
3. 15 cards
4. 24 pencils

page 54

1. $6
2. $7
3. 40 boxes
4. 3 packs
5. 20 plants

page 55

1. 75
2. 200
3. 8
4. 12 minutes
5. 125
6. 27 minutes
7. 15 ribbons
8. 3 minutes

page 56

1. $4
2. $2
3. record
4. car
5. $15
6. $12
7. 2 cars
8. 3 airplanes

page 57

Student drawings may vary. Be sure they accurately represent the problems.
1. 20 trees
2. 11 trees
3. 10 trees

page 58

1. 3
2. $2
3. 4
4. $3
5. $18
6. $6
7. $12
8. $9

page 59

1. Problem has been completed for students.
2. Student art should show a horizontal line separating 4 and 7 from 3 and 8.
3. Student art should show a vertical line separating 1, 5, and 3 from 2, 3, and 4.
4. Student art should show a horizontal line separating 8 and 2 from 5, 2, and 3.
5. Student art should show a slanted line separating 4 and 7 from 1, 5, 3, and 2.

page 60

1. 3 points
2. $5
3. 4 pans
4. 6 hours
5. 8 stamps

page 61

1. pear 20¢, banana 10¢
2. pen 99¢, pencil 20¢, eraser 25¢
3. puzzle $2, record $1, book $3
4. bone $1, dog dish $3, collar $4

page 62

1. 10¢
2. 72¢
3. 14 cups
4. 12 pies
5. 6 boxes

page 63

1. 60¢
2. 45¢
3. 2
4. 10
5. 10¢
6. 7¢
7. $1
8. $3

page 64

1. 4 rows
2. 4 tomatoes
3. 8 days
4. 6 hills